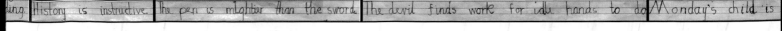

Timeline of Victorian education

1833-1850

Parliament passes a series of laws limiting the hours that children and young adults can work in mines and factories.

1850

The government encourages towns to open free public libraries. The first opens in Manchester in 1852.

1844

The Ragged Schools Union is founded to provide free education to poor children in British cities.

1861

A government report warns that teaching standards in England are low and many children do not go to school at all.

1870

Elementary Education Act:
school boards are encouraged
to build new schools in areas
that do not have enough
school places.

1891

Parents no longer have to
pay for their children's
elementary education.

1872

In Scotland, schooling is
made compulsory for
children between 5 and 13.

1893, 1899

The school leaving age is
increased to 11, then 12.

1880

A new Elementary Education
Act for England and Wales
makes school compulsory for
children aged 5–10. Parents
have to pay a small weekly fee.

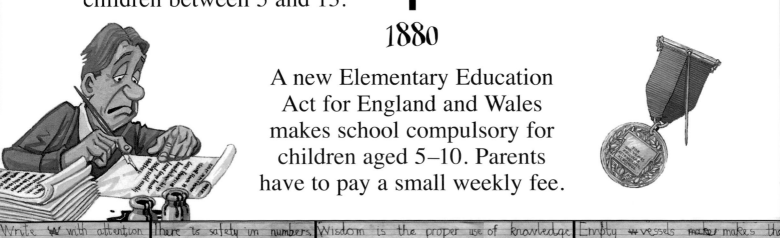

Author:

John Malam studied ancient history and archaeology at the University of Birmingham, after which he worked as an archaeologist at the Ironbridge Gorge Museum, Shropshire. He is now an author, specialising in information books for children. He lives in Cheshire with his wife, a book designer, and their two children. Website: www.johnmalam.co.uk

Artist:

David Antram was born in Brighton, England, in 1958. He studied at Eastbourne College of Art and then worked in advertising for 15 years before becoming a full-time artist. He has illustrated many children's non-fiction books.

Series creator:

David Salariya was born in Dundee, Scotland. He has illustrated a wide range of books and has created and designed many new series for publishers both in the U.K. and overseas. In 1989 he established The Salariya Book Company. He lives in Brighton with his wife, illustrator Shirley Willis, and their son Jonathan.

Editor:

Karen Barker Smith

Assistant Editor:

Stephanie Cole

Dedicated to the staff and children of Leaf Lane Infants School, Winsford, Cheshire.

Handwriting by Jonathan Salariya.

Published in Great Britain in MMXIV by Book House, an imprint of The Salariya Book Company Ltd 25 Marlborough Place, Brighton BN1 1UB www.salariya.com

PB ISBN-13: 978-1-909645-28-8

SALARIYA
SCRIBO BOOK HOUSE SCRIBBLERS

9 8

A CIP catalogue record for this book is available from the British Library.

Printed and bound in China. Printed on paper from sustainable sources. Reprinted in MMXX.

Visit
www.salariya.com
for our online catalogue and **free** fun stuff.

PAPER FROM

SUSTAINABLE
FORESTS

You Wouldn't Want to Be a Victorian Schoolchild!

Written by
John Malam

Created and designed by
David Salariya

Illustrated by
David Antram

Lessons you'd rather not learn

BOOK HOUSE
a SALARIYA imprint

Contents

Introduction

t is the year 1887 and Her Majesty Queen Victoria has ruled the United Kingdom of Great Britain for 50 glorious years. You are fortunate to be living in this modern age. It is a time of rapid progress, when steam trains cross the country at terrifying speed, towns are growing into great industrial cities and you have the right to be educated. If you had been a child from an ordinary working class family at the start of Queen Victoria's reign, education would have been the last thing on your mind. You would have been expected to earn your keep, working for a few pennies a week. The chances are you wouldn't have learned how to read, write or count.

However, in the 1870s, laws were passed stating that all children – not just those from upper class families – should have a proper education. Thousands of new

schools were built and in 1880 it became compulsory for all children between the ages of 5 and 10 to go to school. You have to go because it is now the law of the land. It's no use thinking you can sneak off from school – the teachers have ways of catching truants. And if it is your bad luck to have an incredibly strict headteacher, then you wouldn't want to be a Victorian schoolchild at all!

5

School – the place for you
Ready for school:

SLEEP WELL the night before school starts so you don't come to lessons tired. Yawning in class will land you in trouble.

WASH PROPERLY before you come to school. Scruffy urchins will be sent home.

EAT A GOOD BREAKFAST. An empty stomach is as bad as an empty head at school.

DON'T BE LATE. School starts at 9 o'clock sharp. If you're late you'll be sent to see the headteacher for a telling-off.

Listen out for the school bell at the start of each new day, calling all children to their lessons. Your brand new school is called a Board School because your town's Board of Education built it. The school is a modern red brick building with room for around 1,500 pupils. Boys and girls don't mix much at school so they have separate entrances. It's almost like two schools in one building – one school for the boys and another for the girls.

SCHOOL PENCE. Education won't be free of charge until 1891. Until then you'll pay 2 pence (2d) a week.

Victorian pennies

I won't go!

Get into that school, now!

6

School begins at 9 o'clock!

Who's who:

HEADTEACHERS.
There are three: a headmaster for the boys, a headmistress for the girls and a head of infants.

TEACHERS.
Men teach boys, women teach girls. You call a male teacher 'Sir' and a female teacher 'Miss' or 'Madam'.

PUPIL TEACHERS.
Older pupils sometimes help to teach younger pupils.

ATTENDANCE OFFICER.
If you play truant, this is the man who will catch you.

SCHOOL INSPECTOR.
He visits the school to check up on the teachers and pupils.

Once you're through the school gates you will be in school for the rest of the day. If you get there early, you'll have some time to meet your friends – and enemies – in the playground. As 9 o'clock approaches you are called into the school building by a teacher ringing a handbell. Get a move on – don't dawdle!

What a lovely bunch...

BOING!

twang!

8

The first thing you must do is go to the school hall for assembly. There are separate assemblies for boys and for girls. Stand still, stand in line and most of all, be quiet! Face the front and pay attention as the headteacher leads the assembly. You will say the Lord's Prayer and sing some hymns. If there are any announcements to be made, this is when the headteacher will make them.

Handy hint

There are no smelly toilets inside the school building. They're outside in the fresh air. It's a good idea to go before lessons begin.

NIT NURSE. When assembly is over you'll be inspected by the nit nurse. If she finds lice in your hair, she will shave your head.

ILLNESS. Don't come to school with infectious diseases such as chicken pox or measles. If you do, you'll be sent straight back home.

pong!

CLEANLINESS. Make an effort to look clean. If you insist on looking like you've been rolling in mud, you will be sent to the washroom or maybe even home.

9

'Here Miss!' In the classroom

Around the classroom:

BLACKBOARD. The teacher writes on the blackboard with chalk. It's on wheels and can be moved around.

SCHOOL DESK. You have to share your desk with another pupil. It's made from wood and iron.

Blackboard

Assembly finishes at 9.30, and you file back to your classroom: boys to their room and girls to theirs. Go straight to your desk and sit down. Be quick and don't make a noise! When everyone is in place your teacher will call out the class register in alphabetical order. When you hear your name, answer in a loud, clear voice: 'Here, Miss!'. If you mumble or if she sees you fidgeting, messing with your inkwell or fiddling with your desk, she'll shake the school signal to attract your attention. When the register has been called out, it will be time for the first lesson of the day to begin.

Slate pencil

Slate

REGISTER. Everyone's name is in the register. If you're present, the teacher writes a ✔. If you're absent she writes a ✗.

Register

Desk

WRITING EQUIPMENT. You do most of your schoolwork on a piece of thin slate, which is a type of stone. You write on it with a slate pencil. Young children learn to write using a sand tray.

Sand tray

10

SCHOOL SIGNAL. You'll know when the teacher uses the signal because you'll hear the sharp clicking sound it makes. The headteachers' signals make the loudest clicks of all.

Signal

rattle!

Handy hint

Stand up as soon as an adult comes into the classroom. This shows respect for your elders and betters. If you don't stand up, you'll be in trouble.

Pay attention, girl!

She's seen you!

'Open your readers!'
The reading lesson

Are you ready for this?

LEARN BY HEART. You have to learn pages and pages of text off by heart, especially poems. Then you'll be asked to recite them from memory.

KNOW THE ALPHABET. You should have learned the alphabet at infants' school, from A to Z. If you didn't, you'll struggle with the reading lesson.

After the register has been called, the first lesson begins: reading. It's one of the lessons known as the 'three Rs', reading, 'riting and 'rithmetic. They're the most important parts of your education.

Speak up, boy!

S-s-sorry, S-s-s-sir!

eeerrrm...

Jj Jay
Kk King
Ll Lion
Mm Miser
Nn Nurse
Oo Owl
Pp
Qq Queen
Rr Raven

12

At the beginning of the lesson, a monitor will hand a book, called a reader, to everyone in the class. It's written especially for children, with lots of short, simple sentences. You might be called to the front of the classroom. Take your reader with you. The teacher will ask you to read out loud to the class and the other children will follow the story in their books. Read clearly and carefully – if you make any mistakes the teacher will tell you to try again until you get it right.

Handy hint

blink blink

If you've got bad eyesight, make sure you sit at the front of the classroom. This way you'll be able to see the blackboard and read the wall charts.

13

'No blots!' The writing lesson

What you will need:

COPYBOOK. This is what you write in. It might be especially printed for schools, like this one, or it could be a plain exercise book.

Copybooks

RULER AND PENCIL. Make sure your pencil is sharp and your ruler straight.

Ruler

Pencil

Pen

Inkwell

PEN AND INK. You write with a pen that has a hard, steel nib which you dip into your inkwell. Ink is messy stuff – try not to get it on your hands or clothes.

Each lesson lasts about half an hour. When the reading lesson ends, you are told to get ready for the writing lesson. You'll need a ruler and pencil, a pen and, most important of all, your writing book or copybook. The teacher tells you to open your copybook at a clean page and rule some neat, straight lines on it. A monitor fills a tray of inkwells with bluey-black ink and gives one to each child in the class. Observe the teacher as she writes a sentence on the blackboard. You must copy it word for word in your best handwriting into your copybook.

Miss Battleaxe

Handy hint

Don't put too much ink on the nib of your pen. If you do you'll blot your copybook with ink spots.

Ink monitor

Ooops!

Now you've blotted my copybook!

SIT UP STRAIGHT!
If the teacher thinks you're a lazy child who is not trying hard enough, she might make you sit with a back straightener pressed into your back. It'll make you sit up and concentrate.

15

'Times tables!' The arithmetic lesson

Teachers will tell you that arithmetic is the most important of the 'three Rs' but you may not agree with them. They want you to be able to add and subtract, divide and multiply. Most of all they want you to do sums in your head, which is why it's called mental arithmetic. You'll also learn about fractions, percentages, decimals and something called interest, which is very important if you want to make lots of money when you start work. And if you think this lot sounds difficult, just wait until the teacher starts filling your head with algebra and geometry!

It's all part of the lesson:

ABACUS. You do your sums using a ball frame or abacus. You can thank the ancient Greeks and Romans for this counting contraption – and you know what happened to them!

MENTAL ARITHMETIC. Your fingers will come in handy for this!

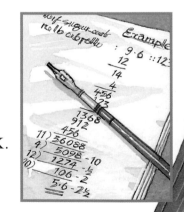

MATHS BOOK. This is the exercise book you write in.

KNOW YOUR NUMBERS. You are expected to use numbers up to one million!

BAD LUCK, BOYS! The school rules say that boys should be given harder arithmetic than girls.

'What is it?' The object lesson

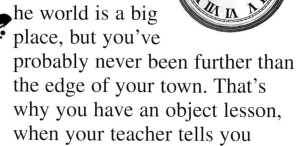

Other lessons:

HISTORY. Colourful wall charts help you learn what life was like in the past.

GEOGRAPHY. Globes and atlases are used to teach you about the countries of the world and Britain's great empire.

GENERAL KNOWLEDGE. In this lesson you are taught some totally useless facts, such as: a duck's quack doesn't echo and starfish don't have brains.

The world is a big place, but you've probably never been further than the edge of your town. That's why you have an object lesson, when your teacher tells you about the world you live in. The school has a specimen cabinet, which is a wooden box filled with lots of objects, from rocks and minerals to dead insects and dried plants. In the object lesson you learn what things are made from, how they work and what they feel and smell like. It's a science lesson.

clever clogs

I think I'm going to faint!

Please can I hold it?

18

Wall chart

Observe this beautiful spider.

Handy hint

Which animal has no brain?

You have textbooks called catechisms which have no pictures in them, just lots of questions and answers. Memorise them all. You'll be asked about them in your tests.

Specimen cabinet

Yuk – it's disgusting!

'Hooray!' It's lunch time

Watch out:

SCHOOL BULLY. Every school has a bully – an older boy (or girl) who picks on children smaller and younger than themselves. Keep your distance is the best advice!

Morning lessons finish at midday. You'll know when that is because monitors walk along the school's corridors ringing handbells. When your desks are tidy the teacher tells the class to leave the classroom – lunch time then begins. You will now have two hours to eat your lunch, play games and if you're not careful, get picked on by the school bully. Most children go home for lunch but some bring sandwiches and fruit to eat.

Aaaarrghh!

Hee hee!

Skipping

rattle rattle

Hoop and stick

20

Lunch time is when you can meet up with your friends and your foes. It's a time of fun and fights, bumps and bruises. A teacher will be on duty in the playground. If he sees anyone misbehaving, he'll blow a whistle.

Who wants to play?

Handy hint
Yum!

The bully might be after your food. Make sure you eat it, not him!

CHASE. Anyone can join in – it always ends up with boys chasing girls.

MARBLES. This is a game of skill – if your marble hits your opponent's, you keep his.

HOOP AND STICK. You roll an iron hoop around the playground – see who can keep it going longest.

SKIPPING. This is a game for girls – they chant rhymes as they jump up and down with their skipping rope.

FOOTBALL. Boys play this with a hard, heavy ball made from leather.

Football

Yuk! Fish paste sandwiches!

gulp!

Screeeech!

Chase

Marbles

'Back to school!' Afternoon lessons

essons start again at 2 o'clock. Go straight to your classroom and sit down at your desk. To make sure that everyone has come back to school, the teacher will call out the class register, just like at the start of the morning lessons. Afternoon lessons are often the same as the morning ones – more reading, 'riting and 'rithmetic. There are also practical lessons, such as the drill lesson. It will improve your fitness through lots of running around, jumping up and down, climbing ropes and touching your toes. On your marks, get set, go!

Pant!

Your toes – not mine, stupid!

Afternoon lessons:

THREE Rs AGAIN. Stop day-dreaming! If you can't read, write or add and subtract then you won't do well in your tests.

HYGIENE. You're taught about personal hygiene – how to keep yourself clean and why it's important to do so.

HOUSEWORK AND COOKERY. Girls are taught 'domestic science' which is how to look after the house and home.

SINGING. In this lesson you will learn traditional songs and hymns, as well as all five verses of *God Save the Queen.*

22

DRAWING. This is a
technical subject, for
boys only. They're
taught how to make
drawings of buildings
and parts for machines.

23

Prizes and punishments

The bad are punished:

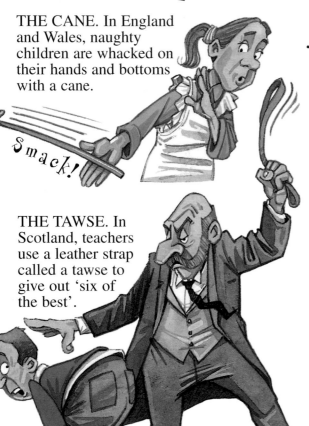

THE CANE. In England and Wales, naughty children are whacked on their hands and bottoms with a cane.

Smack!

THE TAWSE. In Scotland, teachers use a leather strap called a tawse to give out 'six of the best'.

LINES. This is a much less painful punishment! You'll be told to write the same sentence out 100 times or more!

Afternoon lessons finish at 5 o'clock. Monitors walk along the school corridors ringing handbells to announce the end of the school day. Inside each classroom, ink monitors collect inkwells from the desks and you are told to tidy your writing slates and books away. Then you stand, say prayers, leave the room in a quiet and orderly fashion and go home. However, if you've been naughty during the day you'll be told to stay behind. Off you'll go to the headteacher's study to be punished. He'll write the details of your bad behaviour and punishment in his log book, which is like a diary.

The good are rewarded:

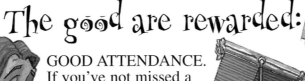

GOOD ATTENDANCE. If you've not missed a single day at school in the whole year, you'll be given a medal.

CERTIFICATES. If you've done good work you'll be rewarded with a certificate.

BOOKS. Once a year, there is a prize day, when books are given to children who've done well at school.

24

'Test time!' Inspection day

One of the school's most important days is inspection day. It's not just pupils that are inspected, but school buildings, equipment and, most of all, how good the teachers are at their jobs. How do the inspectors check the teachers? By giving you a test! If lots of children fail, the teachers will be in trouble.

Surely she'll get that right!

Not that old question again...

Can you name an animal that has no brain?

Children are tested one at a time. You're called to meet the inspectors and they ask you some tricky questions about the subjects you've been studying. If you've worked hard all year you should have no difficulty with the test. But if you've been absent a lot – because of illness or because you've played truant – the test won't be so easy.

Handy hint

Don't miss inspection day! If you're ill, someone will come for you.

Have you passed your tests?

YES. Well done! You'll be given a certificate that says which subjects you've been tested in and have passed. You can now move up to the next Standard or class.

A starfish, Sir!

One day I'll get out of here...

NO. Bad luck. You'll have to stay in the same class until it's time to take the test again in a year's time. You might be the oldest child in the class.

End of term treats

> I think I'll be an actor when I grow up.

Here's the good news – school is not all hard work. For a start, you have Saturdays off (on Sundays, you go to Sunday school, organised by your church). You also have two weeks holiday at Christmas and Easter and six weeks in the summer, as well as time off for May Day and Whitsuntide.

The end of the school year is a busy time. There will be sports day, an outing, and visitors will come to the school with puppet shows. The end of year highlight will be the school play – perhaps you'll be picked for a starring role. One thing's for sure, children everywhere will be heard chanting, *'No more Latin, no more French, no more sitting on a hard school bench!'*

Fun at school:

SPORTS DAY. You'll take part in games such as the sack race and the egg-and-spoon race. Do your best to win!

MAGIC LANTERN SHOW. A projector, or lantern, will shine colourful pictures of faraway places and animals onto a screen. It'll seem like magic!

28

Handy hint

In the summer holidays you might have to help with the harvest. Make the most of it before the new term starts!

I need a holiday, too!

SCHOOL TRIP. If you're really lucky, you'll be taken by steam train into the countryside for a picnic, or to the seaside where you can make sandcastles on the beach.

PUNCH AND JUDY. A puppet theatre might visit the school. A little booth will be set up in the playground and you'll gather round it to watch the show.

Glossary

Abacus A frame with balls that move along wires. It is used for counting.

Atlas A book which has maps of all the countries in the world in it.

Back straightener A device worn by children to make them sit up and pay attention.

Board School A school built as a result of the 1870 Elementary Education Act (England and Wales) and the 1872 Scottish Elementary Education Act. Thousands were built across Britain.

Cane A stick used to beat a child.

Catechism A book without pictures, or a method of teaching that uses questions and answers.

Copybook A book in which a schoolchild wrote sentences copied word for word from examples. Copybooks could also be used to copy drawings.

Currency The money which is used in a country.

Drill The name given to the PE (physical education) lesson.

Dunce A person who is slow to learn something.

Empire A group of countries which is ruled by one other country or State.

Foe Another word for enemy.

Handbell A bell that is small enough to carry and ring with one hand.

Hygiene The things you should do to stay clean and healthy.

I hate lines.

30

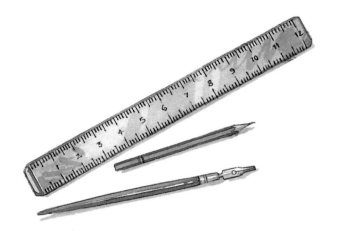

Infectious The word used to describe a disease which can easily be passed from one person to another.

Inkwell A small pot for holding ink.

Log book The school diary, filled in by the headteacher.

Mental arithmetic Working out the answers to sums in your head.

Monitor A child who is given a duty to perform, such as filling the class inkwells.

Reader A textbook which helped schoolchildren learn how to read.

School signal A rattle used to attract a child's attention.

Shilling An old coin which used to be used in Britain.

Standard The name for a class, such as Standard 3, Standard 6 and so on.

Truant A child who misses school without good reason.

Urchin A young, mischievous and messily dressed child.

Whitsuntide A religious holiday approximately seven weeks after Easter.

31

Index

Top Victorian novels about school

It is often said that your schooldays are the best days of your life, but some of the schools described by Victorian novelists were very grim indeed…

Charles Dickens described some truly dreadful schools in his novels. He wrote not just to entertain his readers, but to persuade politicians to improve things.

In *Nicholas Nickleby* (1839), Nicholas is sent to Dotheboys Hall in Yorkshire, where the cruel and ignorant Wackford Squeers is headmaster. The school is finally closed when Squeers is convicted of fraud.

Hard Times (1854), set in a northern industrial town, features the headmaster Mr Gradgrind, who deals only in facts and numbers, and tries to squeeze all imagination out of his pupils.

The novelist **Charlotte Brontë** was a teacher herself for a while.

In *Jane Eyre* (1847) she describes a charity school for girls where the pupils' health is neglected and many of them fall ill; Jane's best friend dies in her arms.

Tom Brown's School Days (1857), by **Thomas Hughes**, is set in a real school – Rugby, a leading public school – and features Rugby's real-life headmaster, Dr Thomas Arnold. Young Tom is tormented by the bully Flashman, but eventually overcomes him and grows up to be a fine, upstanding Victorian gentleman.

Education for all

At the beginning of the Victorian age, education was not for everyone. The rich and powerful sent their sons to the great public schools such as Eton, Harrow or Winchester, while the sons of the middle classes could get a useful education at grammar school.

Girls, if their parents could afford it, might be taught at home by a governess – a female servant who lived with the family. They would learn basic skills such as reading and writing, and ladylike subjects such as French or music.

Small children might attend a 'dame school', run by an elderly woman in her own home. These schools aimed to teach the 'three Rs' and other practical skills. However, a survey carried out in 1838 found that the standard of teaching was often very low.

Many poorer children had no schooling at all. Some worked full-time on farms or in mines or factories. Others led a life of crime, as Charles Dickens described in his novel *Oliver Twist* (1839).

In the early 1840s, 'ragged schools' were set up by volunteers in many industrial cities to provide free education for the very poor. The Earl of Shaftesbury became president of the Ragged Schools Union, and Dickens was a supporter. Children's working hours were gradually reduced, so that they could have time to go to school. But the compulsory free schooling that we take for granted today did not arrive until 1891 – just 10 years before the end of Queen Victoria's reign.

Equal opportunities

Queen's College, London was founded in 1848 by Frederick Denison Maurice as a place where women could study serious academic subjects and earn proper qualifications. Frances Buss and Dorothea Beale were two of its most famous students.

Frances Mary Buss (1827–1894) believed passionately that girls as well as boys should have the chance of a good education. She founded the North London Collegiate School in 1850 and the Camden School for Girls in 1871. She was the first person to use the title 'headmistress'.

Dorothea Beale (1831–1906) was headmistress of Cheltenham Ladies' College, and in 1893 founded St Hilda's College, Oxford. St Hilda's was the last women-only college at Oxford University: it finally allowed men to join in 2008.

Miss Buss and Miss Beale were also suffragists – people who campaigned for women to have the right to vote. Neither of them ever married, and this inspired some unknown wit to write a famous verse about them:

> Miss Buss and Miss Beale
> Cupid's darts do not feel.
> How different from us,
> Miss Beale and Miss Buss!

(Cupid, the Roman god of love, was said to make people fall in love by shooting arrows at them.)

Did you know?

- Many Victorians believed that educating girls would damage their health.

- Others feared that sending working-class children to school would give them dangerous ideas.

For all the stuff you'd rather not know!

You will find loads of free stuff at: youwouldntwantto.be